Ballads and Other Poems

Henry Wadsworth Longfellow

Contents

THE SKELETON IN AEMOUR.	7
THE WRECK OF THE HESPERUS.	14
THE LUCK OF EDENHALL. FROM THE GERMAN OF VHLAND	17
THE ELECTED KNIGHT. FROM THE DANISH.	19
THE CHILDREN OF THE LORD'S SUPPER.	21
THE VILLAGE BLACKSMITH.	33
THE TWO LOCKS OF HAIR. FROM THE GERMAN OF PFIZER.	36
IT IS NOT ALWAYS MAY. NO HAY PAJAROS EN LOS NID0S DE AHTANO.	38
THE RAINY DAY.	39
GOD'S-ACRE.	39
THE GOBLET OF LIFE.	42
MAIDENHOOD.	44
EXCELSIOR.	46

BALLADS AND OTHER POEMS

BY

Henry Wadsworth Longfellow

THE SKELETON IN AEMOUR.

[THE following Ballad was suggested to me while riding on the seashore at Newport. A year or two previous a skeleton had been dug up at Fall River, clad in broken and cor-roded armour; and the idea occurred to me of connecting it with the Round Tower at Newport, generally known hitherto as the Old Wind-Mill, though now claimed by the Danes as a work of their early ancestors. Professor Rafn, in the Mimoires de la Société Royale des Antiquaires du Nord for 1838-1839, says;

" There is no mistaking in this instance the style in which the more ancient stone edifices of the North were constructed, the style which belongs to the Roman or Ante-Gothic architecture, and which, especially after the time of Charlemagne, diffused itself from Italy over the whole of the West and North of Europe, where it continued to predominate until the close of the 12th century; that style, which some authors have, from one of its most striking characteristics, called the round arch style, the same which in England is denominated Saxon and sometimes Norman architecture.

" On the ancient structure in Newport there are no ornaments remaining, which might possibly have served to guide us in assigning the probable date of its erection. That no vestige whatever is found of the pointed arch, nor any approximation to it, is indicative of an earlier rather than of a later period. From such characteristics as remain, however, we can scarcely form any other inference than one, in which I am persuaded that all, who are familiar with Old-Northern architecture, will concur, THAT THIS BUILDING WAS ERECTED AT A PERIOD DECIDEDLY NOT LATER THAN THE 12TH CENTURY. This remark applies, of course, to the original building only, and not to the alterations that it subsequently re-ceived ; for there are several such alterations in the upper part of the building which cannot be mistaken, and which were most likely occasioned by its being adapted in modern times to various uses, for example as the substructure of a wind-mill, and latterly as a hay magazine. To the same times may be referred the windows, the fire-place, and the apertures made above the columns. That this building could not have been erected for a wind-mill, is what an architect will easily discern."

I will not enter into a discussion of the point. It is sufficiently well established for the purpose of a ballad ; though doubtless many an honest citizen of Newport, who has passed his days within sight of the Round Tower, will be ready to exclaim with Sancho; " God bless me! did I not warn you to have a care of what you were doing, for that it was nothing but a wind-mill and nobody could mistake it, but one who had the like in his head."]

" SPEAK ! speak ! thou fearful guest!
 Who, with thy hollow breast
 Still in rude armour drest,
Comest to daunt me!
Wrapt not in Eastern balms,
But with thy fleshless palms
Stretched, as if asking alms,
Why dost thou haunt me?
Then, from those cavernous eyes
Pale flashes seemed to rise,
As when the Northern skies
Gleam in December;
And, like the water's flow
Under December's snow,
Came a dull voice of woe
From the heart's chamber.

" I was a Viking old !
My deeds, though manifold,

No Skald in song has told,
No Saga taught thee !
Take heed, that in thy verse
Thou dost the tale rehearse,
Else dread a dead man's curse !
For this I sought thee.

" Far in the Northern Land,
By the wild Baltic's strand;
I, with my childish hand,
Tamed the ger-falcon;
And, with my skates fast-bound,
Skimmed the half-frozen Sound,
That the poor whimpering hound
Trembled to walk on.

" Oft to his frozen lair
Tracked I the grisly bear,
While from my path the hare
Fled like a shadow;
Oft through the forest dark
Followed the were-wolf's bark, Until the soaring lark
Sang from the meadow,

" But when I older grew,
Joining a corsair's crew,
O'er the dark sea I flew
With the marauders.
Wild was the life we led;
Many the souls that sped,
Many the hearts that bled,
By our stern orders.

" Many a wassail-bout
Wore the long Winter out;
Often our midnight shout
Set the cocks crowing,
As we the Berserk's tale
Measured in cups of ale,
Draining the oaken pail,
Filled to o'erflowing.

" Once as I told in glee
Tales of the stormy sea,
Soft eyes did gaze on me,
Burning yet tender;
And as the white stars shine
On the dark Norway pine,
On that dark heart of mine
Fell their soft splendor.

" I wooed the blue-eyed maid,
Yielding, yet half afraid,
And in the forest's shade
Our vows were plighted.
Under its loosened vest
Fluttered her little breast,
Like birds within their nest
By the hawk frighted.

" Bright in her father's hall
Shields gleamed upon the wall,
Loud sang the minstrels all,
Chaunting his glory;
When of old Hildebrand
I asked his daughter's hand,

Mute did the minstrels stand
To hear my story.

" While the brown ale he quaffed,
Loud then the champion laughed,
And as the wind-gusts waft
The sea-foam brightly,
So the loud laugh of scorn,
Out of those lips unshorn,
From the deep drinking-horn
Blew the foam lightly.

" She was a Prince's child,
I but a Viking wild,
And though she blushed and smiled
I was discarded!
Should not the dove so white
Follow the sea-mew's flight,
Why did they leave that night
Her nest unguarded?

" Scarce had I put to sea,
Bearing the maid with me,—
Fairest of all was she
Among the Norsemen! —
When on the white sea-strand,
Waving his armed hand,
Saw we old Hildebrand,
With twenty horsemen.

" Then launched they to the blast,
Bent like a reed each mast,
Yet we were gaining fast,

When the wind failed us;
And with a sudden flaw
Came round the gusty Skaw,
So that our foe we saw
Laugh as he hailed us.

" And as to catch the gale
Round veered the flapping sail,
Death! was the helmsman's hail,
Death without quarter!
Mid-ships with iron keel
Struck we her ribs of steel;
Down her black hulk did reel
Through the black water!

" As with his wings aslant,
Sails the fierce cormorant,
Seeking some rocky haunt,
With his prey laden,
So toward the open main,
Beating to sea again,
Through the wild hurricane,
Bore I the maiden.

" Three weeks we westward bore,
And when the storm was o'er,
Cloud-like we saw the shore
Stretching to lea-ward;
There for my lady's bower
Built I the lofty tower,
Which, to this very hour,
Stands looking sea-ward.

" There lived we many years;
Time dried the maiden's tears;
She had forgot her fears,
She was a mother;
Death closed her mild blue eyes,
Under that tower she lies;
Ne'er shall the sun arise
On such another !

"Still grew my bosom then,
Still as a stagnant fen!
Hateful to me were men,
The sun-light hateful!
In the vast forest here,
Clad in my warlike gear,
Fell I upon my spear,
O, death was grateful!

" Thus, seamed with many scars
Bursting these prison bars,
Up to its native stars
My soul ascended!
There from the flowing bowl
Deep drinks the warrior's soul,
Skoal ! to the Northland ! **skoal!**" [2]
— Thus the tale ended.

[2] In Scandanavia this is the customary salutation when drinking a health. I have slightly changed the orthography of the word, in order to preserve the correct pronunciation.

THE WRECK OF THE HESPERUS.

IT was the schooner Hesperus,
That sailed the wintry sea;
And the skipper had taken his little daughter,
To bear him company.

Blue were her eyes as the fairy-flax,
Her cheeks like the dawn of day,
And her bosom white as the hawthorn buds,
That ope in the month of May.

The skipper he stood beside the helm,
With his pipe in his mouth,
And watched how the veering flaw did blow
The smoke now West, now South.

Then up and spake an old Sailòr,
Had sailed the Spanish Main,
"I pray thee, put into yonder port,
For I fear a hurricane.
" Last night, the moon had a golden ring,
And to-night no moon we see !"
The skipper, he blew a whiff from his pipe,
And a scornful laugh laughed he.

Colder and louder blew the wind,
A gale from the Northeast;
The snow fell hissing in the brine,
And the billows frothed like yeast.

Down came the storm, and smote amain,
The vessel in its strength;
She shuddered and paused, like a frighted steed,
Then leaped her cable's length.

" Come hither ! come hither ! my little daughtér,
And do not tremble so;
For I can weather the roughest gale,
That ever wind did blow."

He wrapped her warm in his seaman's coat
Against the stinging blast;
He cut a rope from a broken spar,
And bound her to the mast.

" O father! I hear the church-bells ring,
O say, what may it be ?
" " 'T is a fog-bell on a rock-bound coast! "--

And he steered for the open sea.

" O father ! I bear the sound of guns,
O say, what may it be ? " " Some ship in distress, that cannot live
In such an angry sea ! "

"O father ! I see a gleaming light,
O say, what may it be ? "
But the father answered never a word,
A frozen corpse was he.

Lashed to the helm, all stiff and stark,
With his face to the skies,
The lantern gleamed through the gleaming snow

On his fixed and glassy eyes.

Then the maiden clasped her hands and prayed
That saved she might be;
And she thought of Christ, who stilled the wave,
On the Lake-of Galilee.

And fast through the midnight dark and drear,
Through the whistling sleet and snow,
Like a sheeted ghost, the vessel swept
Towards the reef of Norman's Woe,

And ever the fitful gusts between
A sound came from the land ;
It was the sound of the trampling surf,
On the rocks and the hard sea-sand.

The breakers were right beneath her bows,
.She drifted a dreary wreck,
And a whooping billow swept the crew
Like icicles from her deck.

She struck where the white and fleecy waves
Looked soft as carded wool,
But the cruel rocks, they gored her side
Like the horns of an angry bull.

Her rattling shrouds, all sheathed in ice,
With the masts went by the board ;
Like a vessel of glass, she strove and sank,
Ho ! ho ! the breakers roared !

At daybreak, on the bleak sea-beach,

A fisherman stood aghast,
To see the form of a maiden fair,
Lashed close to a drifting mast.

The salt sea was frozen on her breast,
The salt tears in her eyes;
And he saw her hair, like the brown sea-weed,
On the billows fall and. rise.

Such was the wreck of the Hesperus,
In the midnight and the snow !
Christ save us all from a death like this,
On the reef of Norman's Woe !

THE LUCK OF EDENHALL.
FROM THE GERMAN OF VHLAND

[The tradition, upon which this ballad is founded, and the " shards of the Luck of Edenhall," still exist in England. The goblet is in the possession of Sir Christopher Musgrave,. Bart, of Eden Hall, Cumberland; and is not so entirely shat-tered, as the ballad leaves it.]

OF Edenhall, the youthful Lord Bids sound the festal trumpet's call; He rises at the banquet board, And cries, 'mid the drunken revellers all, " Now bring me the Luck of Edenhall!"

The butler hears the words with pain,
The house's oldest seneschal,
Takes slow from its silken cloth again
The drinking glass of crystal tall;
They call it The Luck of Edenhall.

Then said the Lord; " This glass to praise,
Fill with red wine from Portugal!"
The gray-beard with trembling hand obeys ;
A purple light shines over all,
It beams from the Luck of Edenhall.

Then speaks the lord, and it light
"This glass of flashing crystal tall
Gave to my sires the Fountain sprite
She wrote in it ; If this glass doth fall
Farewell then O Luck of Edenhatl

" 'T was right a goblet the Fate should be
Of the joyous race of Edenhall!
Deep draughts drink we right willingly;
And willingly ring, with merry call,
Kling ! klang ! to the Luck of Edenhall!"

First rings it deep, and full, and mild,
Like to the song of a nightingale;
Then like the roar of a torrent wild;
Then mutters at last like the thunder's fall,
The glorious Luck of Edenhall.

As the goblet ringing flies apart,
Suddenly cracks the vaulted hall;
And through the rift, the wild flames start;
The guests in dust are scattered all,
With the breaking Luck of Edenhall!

In storms the foe, with fire and sword;
He in the night had scaled the wall,
Slain by the sword lies the youthful Lord,

But holds in his hand the crystal tall,
The shattered Luck of Edenhall.

On the morrow the butler gropes alone,
The gray-beard in the desert hall,
He seeks his Loard's burnt skelton,
He seeks his Lord's burnt skelton,
He seeks in the dismal ruin's fall
The shards of the luck of Edenhall

" The stone wall," saith he, "doth fall aside,
Down must the stately columns fall;
Glass is this earth's Luck and Pride;
In atoms shall fall this earthly ball
One day like the Luck of Edenhall !"

THE ELECTED KNIGHT.
FROM THE DANISH.

[The following strange and somewhat mystical ballad is from Nyerup and Rabbet's ***Danske Viser*** of the Middle Ages. It seems to refer to the first preaching of Christianity in the North, and to the institution of Knight-Errantry. The three maidens I suppose to be Faith,. Hope, and Charity. The irregularities of the original have been carefully preserved in the translation.}

Sir OLUF he rideth over the plain
Full seven miles broad and seven miles,
But never, ah never can meet with the man
A tilt with bim dare ride

He saw under the hill-side
A Knight full well equipped ;

His steed was black, his helm was barred;
He was riding at full speed.

He wore upon his spurs
Twelve little golden birds ;
Anon he spurred his steed with a clang,
And there sat all the birds and sang.

He wore upon his mail
Twelve little golden wheels ;
Anon in eddies the wild wind blew,
And round and round the wheels they flew.

He wore before his breast
A lance that was poised in rest;
And it was sharper than diamond-stone,
It made Sir Oluf's heart to groan.

He wore upon his helm,
A wreath of ruddy gold ;
And that gave him the Maidens Three,
The youngest was fair to behold.

Sir Oluf questioned the Knight eftsoon
If he were come from heaven down ;
" Art thou Christ of Heaven," quoth he,
" So will I yield me unto thee."

"I am not Christ the Great,
Thou shalt not yield thee yet;
I am an Unknown Knight,
Three modest Maidens have me bedight."

" Art thou a Knight elected,
And have three Maidens thee bedight;
So shalt thou ride a tilt this day,
For all the Maidens' honor ! "

The first tilt they together rode
They put their steeds to the test;
The second tilt they together rode,
They proved thetr manhood best.

The third tilt they together rode,
Neither of them would yield ;
The fourth tilt they together rode,
They both fell on the field

Now lie the lords upon the plain,
And their blood runs unto death;
Now sit the Maidens in the high tower,
The youngest sorrows till death.

THE CHILDREN OF THE LORD'S SUPPER.

FROM THE SWEDISH OF BISHOP TEGNER.

THE
CHILDREN OF THE LORD'S SUPPER.

PENTECOST, day of rejoicing, had come. The church of the village
Stood gleaming white in the morning's sheen. On the spire of the belfry,
Tipped with a vane of metal, the friendly flames of the Spring-sun
Glanced like the tongues of fire, beheld by Apos-tles aforetime.

Clear was the heaven and blue, and'May, with

her cap crowned with roses,
Stood in her holiday dress in the fields, and the
wind and the brooklet
Murmured gladness and peace, God's-peace !
With lips rosy-tinted
Whispered the race of the flowers, and merry
on balancing branches
Birds were singing their carol, a jubilant hymn to
the Highest.
Swept and clean was the churchyard. Adorned like a leaf-woven arbour
Stood its old-fashioned gate; and within upon
each cross of iron
Hung was a sweet-scented garland, new twined
by the hands of affection.
Even the dial, that stood on a fountain among the
departed,
(There full a hundred years had it stood,) was embellished with blossoms.

Like to the patriarch hoary, the sage of his kith and the hamlet,
Who on his birth-day is crowned by children and children's children,
So stood the ancient prophet, and mute with his pencil of iron
Marked on the tablet of stone, and measured the swift-changing moment,
While all around at his feet, an eternity slumbered in quiet
Also the church within was adorned, for this was the season
In which the young, their parents' hope, and the loved-ones of heaven,
Should at the foot of the altar renew the vows of their baptism.
Therefore each nook and corner was swept and cleaned, and the dust was
Blown from the walls and ceiling, and from the oil-painted benches.

There stood the church, like a garden; the Feast of the Leafy Pavilions [3]
Saw we in living presentment. From noble arms on the church wall
Grew forth a cluster of leaves, and the preacher's pulpit of oak-wood .
Budded once move anew, as aforetime the rod before Aaron.

Wreathed thereon was the Bible with leaves, and the dove, washed with silver,
Under its canopy fastened, a necklace had on of wind-flowers.
But in front of the choir, round the altar-piece painted by Hörberg,†
Crept a garland gigantic ; and bright-curling tresses of angels

> [3]The Feast of the Tabernacles; in Swedish, Löfhyddo-högtiden, the Leaf-huts'-high-tide.

The peasant-painter of Sweden. He is known chiefly by his altar-pieces in the village churches.

Peeped, like the sun from a cloud, out of the shadowy leaf-work.
Likewise the lustre of brass, new-polished, blinked from the ceiling,
And for lights there were lilies of Pentecost set in the sockets.

Loud rang the bells already; the thronging crowd was assembled
Far from valleys and hills, to list to the holy preaching.
Hark! then roll forth at once the mighty tones from the organ,
Hover like voices from God, aloft like invisible spirits.
Like as Elias in heaven, when he cast off from him his mantle,
Even so cast off the soul its garments of earth;and with one voice

Chimed in the congregation, and sang an anthem immortal
Of the sublime Wallin,[4]of David's harp in the North-land
Tuned to the choral of Luther; the song on its powerful pinions
Took every living soul, and lifted it gently to heaven,
And every face did shine like the Holy One's face upon Tabor.
Lo ! there entered then into the church the Reverend Teacher.
Father he hight and he was in the parish; a christianly plainness
Clothed from his head to his feet the old man of seventy winters.

> [4]A distinguished pulpit-orator and poet. He is particularly remarkable for the beauty and sublimity of his psalms.

Friendly was he to behold, and glad as the heralding angel
Walked he among the crowds, but still a contemplative grandeur
Lay on his forehead as clear, as on moss-covered grave-stone a sun-beam.
As in his inspiration (an evening twilight that faintly
Gleams in the human soul, even now, from the day of creation)
Th' Artist, the friend of heaven, imagines Saint John when in Patmos ;—
Gray, with his eyes uplifted to heaven, so seemed then the old man ;
Such was the glance of his eye, and such were his tresses of silver.
All the congregation arose in the pews that were numbered.
But with a cordial look, to the right and the left hand, the old man
Nodding all hail and peace, disappeared in the innermost chancel.

Simply and solemnly now proceeded the Chris-tian service,
Singing and prayer, and at last an ardent dis-course from the old man.
Many a moving word and warning, that out of the heart came
Fell like the dew of the morning, like manna on those in the desert.
Afterwards, when all was finished, the Teacher reentered the chancel,
Followed therein by the young. On the right hand the boys had their places,
Delicate figures, with close-curling hair and cheeks rosy-blooming.
But on the left-hand of these, there stood the tremulous lilies,
Tinged with the blushing light of the morning, the diffident maidens,—
Folding their hands in prayer, and their eyes cast down on the pavement.
Now came, with question and answer, the cate-chism. In the beginning
Answered the children with troubled and faltering voice, but the old man's
Glances of kindness encouraged them soon, and the doctrines eternal
Flowed, like the waters of fountains, so clear from lips unpolluted.
Whene'er the answer was closed, and as oft as they named the Redeemer,
Lowly louted the boys, and lowly the maidens all courtesied.
Friendly the Teacher stood, like an angel of light there among them,
And to the children explained, he the holy, the highest, in few words,
Thorough, yet simple and clear, for sublimity always is simple,
Both in sermon and song, a child can seize on its meaning.

Even as the green-growing bud is unfolded when Spring-tide approaches
Leaf by leaf is developed, and, warmed by the radiant sunshine,
Blushes with purple and gold, till at last the per-fected blossom
Opens its odorous chalice, and rocks with its crown in the breezes,
So was unfolded here .the Christian lore of sal-vation,
Line by line from the soul of childhood. The fathers and mothers
Stood behind them in tears, and were glad at each well-worded answer.
Now went the old man up to the altar ; and straightway transfigured
(So did it seem unto me) was then the affectionate Teacher.
Like the Lord's Prophet sublime, and awful as Death and as Judgment
Stood he, the God-commissioned, the soul-searcher, earthward descending.
Glances, sharp as a sword, into hearts, that to him were transparent
Shot he; his voice was deep,was low like the thunder afar off.
So on a sudden transfigured he stood there, he spake aud he questioned.

" This is the faith of the Fathers, the faith the Apostles delivered,
This is moreover the faith whereunto I baptized you, while stillye
Lay on your mothers' breasts, and nearer the portals of heaven.
Slumbering received you then the Holy Church in its bosom;
Wakened from sleep are ye now, and the light in its radiant splendor
Rains from the heaven downward; — to-day on the threshold of childhood
Kindly she frees you again, to examine and make your election,
For she knows nought of compulsion, only conviction desireth.
This is the hour of your trial, the turning-point of existence,
Seed for the coming days; without revocation departeth
Now from your lips the confession ; Bethink ye, before ye make answer !
Think not, O think not with guile to deceive the questioning Teacher.
Sharp is his eye to-day, and a curse ever rests upon falsehood.
Enter not with a lie on Life's journey ; the multitude hears you,
Brothers and sisters and parents, what dear upon earth is and holy
Standeth before your sight as a witness; the Judge everlasting
Looks from the sun down upon you, and angels in waiting beside him
Grave your confession in letters of fire, upon tablets eternal.

Thus then, — believe ye in God, in the Father who this world created?
Him who redeemed it, the Son, and the Spirit where both are united?
Will ye promise me here, (a holy promise!) to cherish
God more than all things earthly, and every man as a brother?
Will ye promise me here, to confirm your faith by your living,
Th' heavenly faith of affection! to hope, to forgive, and to suffer,
Be what it may your condition, and walk before God in uprightness?
Will ye promise me this before God and man?" With a clear voice
Answered the young men Yes! and Yes! with lips softly-breathing
Answered the maidens eke. Then dissolved from the brow of the Teacher
Clouds with the thunders therein, and he spake on in accents more gentle,
Soft as the evening's breath, as harps by Babylon's rivers.

" Hail,, then, hail to you all! To the heirdom of heaven be ye welcome!
Children no more from this day, but by covenant brothers and sisters!
Yet, — for what reason not children? Of such is the kingdom of heaven.
Here upon earth an assemblage of children, in heaven one father,
Ruling them as his own household, — forgiving in turn and chastising,
That is of human life a picture, as Scripture has taught us.
Blessed are the pure before God! Upon purity and upon virtue
Resteth the Christian Faith; she herself from on high is descended.
Strong as a man and pure as a child, is the sum of the doctrine,
Which the Godlike delivered, and on the cross suffered and died for.
O! as ye wander this day from childhood's sacred asylum
Downward and ever downward, and deeper in Age's chill valley,
O! how soon will ye come, — too soon! — and long to turn backward
Up to its hill-tops again, to the sun-illumined, where Judgment
Stood like a father before you, and Pardon, clad like a mother,
Gave you her hand to kiss, and the loving heart was forgiven,
Life was a play and your hands grasped after the roses of heaven!
Seventy years have I lived already; the father eternal
Gave to me gladness and care; but the loveliest hours of existence,
When I have steadfastly gazed in their eyes, I have instantly known them,

Known them all, all again; — they were my childhood's acquaintance.
Therefore take from henceforth, as guides in the paths of existence,
Prayer, with her eyes raised to heaven, and Innocence, bride of man's childhood.
Innocence, child beloved, is a guest from the world of the blessed,
Beautiful, and in her hand a lily ; on life's roaring billows
Swings she in safety, she heedeth them not, in the ship she is sleeping.
Calmly she gazes around in the turmoil of men ; in the desert
Angels descend and minister unto her; she herself knoweth
Naught of her glorious attendance ; but follows faithful and humble,
Follows so long as she may her friend; O do not reject her,
For she cometh from God and she holdeth the keys of the heavens.'—
Prayer is Innocence' friend ; and willingly flyeth incessant
'Twixt the earth and the sky, the carrier-pigeon of heaven.
Son of Eternity, fettered in Time, and an exile, the Spirit
Tugs at his chains evermore, and struggles like flames ever upward.
Still he recalls with emotion his father's manifold mansions,
Thinks of the land of his fathers, where blos-somed more freshly the flowers,
Shone a more beautiful sun, and he played with the winged angels.
Then grows the earth too narrow, too close ; and homesick for heaven
Longs the wanderer again; and the Spirit's long-ings are worship ;
Worship is called his most beautiful hour, and its tongue is entreaty.
Ah! when the infinite burden of life descendeth upon us,
Crushes to earth our hope, and, under the earth, in the grave-yard, —
Then it is good to pray unto God ; for his sorrowing children
Turns he ne'er from his door, but he heals and helps and consoles them.
Yet is it better to pray when all things are pros-perous with us,
Pray in fortunate days, for life's most beautiful Fortune
Kneels down before the Eternal's throne; and, with hands interfolded,.
Praises thankful and moved the only giver of blessings.
Or do ye know, ye children, one blessing that comes not from Heaven ?
What has mankind forsooth, the poor ! that it has not received ?
Therefore, fall in the dust and pray ! The seraphs adoring

Cover with pinions six their face in the glory of him who
Hung his masonry pendant on naught, when the world he created.
Earth declareth his might, and the firmament uttereth his glory.
Races blossom and die, and stars fall downward from heaven,
Downward like withered leaves; at the last stroke of midnight, millenniums
Lay themselves down at his feet, and he sees them, but counts them as nothing.
Who shall stand in his presence ? The wrath of the judge is terrific,
Casting the insolent down at a glance. When he speaks in his anger
Hillocks skip like the kid, and mountains leap like the roe-buck.
Yet, why are ye afraid, ye children? This awful avenger,
Ah! is a merciful God ! God's voice was not in the earthquake
Not in the fire, nor the storm, but it was in the whispering breezes.
Love is the root of creation; God's essence; worlds without number
Lie in his bosom like children ; he made them for this purpose only.
Only to love and to be loved again, he breathed forth his spirit
Into the slumbering dust, and upright standing, it laid its
Hand on its heart, and felt it was warm with a flame out of heaven.
Quench, O quench not that flame ! It is the breath of your being.
Love is life, but hatred is death. Not father, nor mother
Loved you, as God has loved you; for't was that you may be happy
Gave he his only son. When he bowed down his head in the death-hour
Solemnized Love its triumph; the sacrifice then was completed.
Lo ! then was rent on a sudden the vail of the temple, dividing
Earth and heaven apart, and the dead from their sepulchres rising
Whispered with pallid lips and low in the ears of each other
Th' answer, but dreamed of before, to creation's enigma, —Atonement!
Depths of Love are Atonement's depths, for Love is Atonement.
Therefore, child of mortality, love thou the mer-ciful Father;
Wish what the Holy One wishes, and not from fear, but affection;
Fear is the virtue of slaves; but the heart that loveth is willing;
Perfect was before God, and perfect is Love, and Love only.
Lovest thou God as thou oughtest, then lovest thou likewise thy brethren;

One is the sun in heaven, and one, only one, is Love also.
Bears not each human figure the godlike stamp on his forehead ?
Readest thou not in his face thine origin ? Is he not sailing
Lost like thyself on an ocean unknown, and is he not guided
By the same stars that guide thee ? Why shouldst thou hate then thy brother ?
Hateth he thee, forgive ! For 't is sweet to stammer one letter
Of the Eternal's language ;on earth it is called Forgiveness!
Knowest thou Him, who forgave, with the crown of thorns round his temples
?

Earnestly prayed for his foes, for his murderers ? Say, dost thou know him ?
Ah ! thou confessest his name, so follow likewise
his example, Think of thy brother no ill, but throw a veil over his failings,
Guide the erring aright; for the good, the heavenly shepherd
Took the lost lamb in his arms, and bore it back to its mother.
This is the fruit of Love, and it is by its fruits that we know it.
Love is the creature's welfare, with God; but Love among mortals
Is but an endless sigh ! He longs, and endures, and stands waiting,
Suffers and yet rejoices, and smiles with tears on his eyelids.
Hope, — so is called upon earth, his recompense. — Hope, the befriending,
Does what she can, for she points evermore up to heaven, and.faithful
Plunges her anchors peak in the depths of the grave, and beneath it
Paints a more beautiful world, a dim, but a sweet play of shadows!
Races, better than we, have leaned on her waver-ing promise,
Having naught else beside Hope. Then praise we our Father in heaven,
Him, who has given us more ; for to us has Hope been illumined,
Groping no longer in night; she is Faith, she is living assurance.
Faith is enlightened Hope ; she is light, is the eye of affection,
Dreams of the longing interprets, and carves their visions in marble.
Faith is die sun of life; and her countenance shines like the Prophet's,
For she has looked upon God; the heaven on its stable foundation
Draws she with chains down to earth, and the New Jerusalem sinketh
Splendid with portals twelve in golden vapors descending.
There enraptured she wanders, and looks at the figures majestic,

Fears not the wingéd crowd, in the midst of them all is her homestead.
Therefore love and believe; for works will follow spontaneous
Even as day does the sun; the Right from the Good is an offspring,
Love in a bodily shape; and Christian works are no more than
Animate Love and faith, as flowers are the animate spring-tide.
Works do follow us all unto God; there stand and bear witness
Not what they seemed,—but what they were only. Blessed is he who
Hears their confession secure; they are mute upon earth until death's hand
Opens the mouth of-the silent. Ye children, does Death e'er alarm you?
Death is the brother of Love, twin-brother is he, and is only
More austere to behold. With a kiss upon lips that are fading
Takes he the soul and departs, and rocked in the arms of affection,
Places the ransomed child, new born, 'fore the face of its father.
Sounds of his coming already I hear,—see dimly his pinions,
Swart as the night, but with stars strewn upon them! I fear not before him.
Death is only release, and in mercy is mute. On his bosom
Freer breathes, in its coolness, my breast; and face to face standing
Look I on God as he is, a sun unpolluted by vapors;
Look on the light of the ages I loved, the spirits majestic,
Nobler, better than I; they stand by the throne all transfigured,
Vested in white, and with harps of gold, and are singing an anthem,
Writ in the climate of heaven, in the language spoken by angels.
You, in like manner, ye children beloved, he one day shall gather,
Never forgets he the weary;—then welcome, ye loved ones, hereafter!
Meanwhile forget not the keeping of vows, forget not the promise,
Wander from holiness onward to holiness; earth shall ye heed not;
Earth is but dust and heaven is light; I have pledged you to heaven.
God of the Universe, hear me! thou fountain of Love everlasting,
Hark to the voice of thy servant! I send up my prayer to thy heaven!
Let me hereafter not miss at thy throne one spirit of all these,
Whom thou hast given me here! I have loved them all like a father.
May they bear witness for me, that I taught them the way of salvation,
Faithful, so far as I knew of thy word; again may they know me,

Ballads and Other Poems

    Fall on their Teacher's breast, and before thy face may I place them,
    Pure as they now are, but only more tried, and exclaiming with gladness,
    Father, lo ! I am here, and the children, whom thou hast given me ! "

    Weeping he spake in these words; and now at the beck of the old man
    Knee against knee they knitted a wreath round the altar's enclosure.
    Kneeling he read then the prayers of the conse-cration, and softly With him the children read; at the close, with tremulous accents,
    Asked he the peace of heaven, a benediction upon them.
    Now should have ended his task for the day; the following Sunday
    Was for the young appointed to eat of the Lord's holy Supper.
    Sudden, as struck from the clouds, stood the Teacher silent and laid his
    Hand on his forehead, and cast his looks upward; while thoughts high and holy
    Flew through the midst of his soul, and his eyes glanced with wonderful bright-ness.
    "On the next Sunday, who knows ! perhaps I shall rest in the grave-yard !
    Some one perhaps of yourselves, a lily broken untimely,
    Bow down his head to the earth ; why delay I ? the hour is accomplished.
    Warm is the heart;—I will so ! for to-day grows the harvest of heaven.
    What I began accomplish I now ; for what failing therein is
    I, the old man, will answer to God and the rev-erend father.
    Say to me only, ye children, ye denizens new-come in heaven,
    Are ye ready this day to eat of the bread of Atonement ?
    What it denoteth, that know ye full well, I have told it you often.
    Of the new covenant a symbol it is, of Atonement a token,
    Stablished between earth and heaven. Man by his sins and transgressions
    Far has wandered from God, from his essence. 'T was in the beginning
    Fast by the Tree of Knowledge he fell, and it hangs its crown o'er the
    Fall to this day; in the Thought is the Fall; in the Heart the Atonement.
    Infinite is the Fall, the Atonement infinite like-wise.
    See ! behind me, as far as the old man remem-bers, and forward,
    Far as Hope in her flight can reach with her wearied pinions,

Sin and Atonement incessant go through the lifetime of mortals.
Brought forth is sin full-grown; but Atonement sleeps in our bosoms
Still as the cradled babe ; and dreams of heaven and of angels,
Cannot awake to sensation; is like the tones in the harp's strings,
Spirits imprisoned, that wait evermore the deliverer's finger.
Therefore, ye children beloved, descended the Prince of Atonement,
Woke the slumberer from sleep, and she stands now with eyes all resplendent,
Bright as the vault of the sky, and battles with Sin and o'ercomes her.
Downward to earth he came and transfigured,thence reascended,
Not from the heart in like wise, for there he still lives in the Spirit,
Loves and atones evermore. So long as Time is, is Atonement.
Therefore with reverence receive this day her visible token.
Tokens are dead if the things do not live. The light everlasting
Unto the blind man is not, but is born of the eye that has vision.
Neither in bread nor in wine, but in the heart that is hallowed
Lieth forgiveness enshrined ; the intention alone of amendment
Fruits of the earth ennobles to heavenly things, and removes all
Sin and the guerdon of sin. Only Love with his arms wide extended,
Penitence weeping and praying ; the Will that is tried, and whose gold flows
Purified forth from the flames ; in a word, mankind by Atonement
Breaketh Atonement's bread, and drinketh Atonement's wine-cup.
But he who cometh up hither, unworthy, with hate in his bosom,
Scoffing at men and at God, is guilty of Christ's blessed body,
And the Redeemer's blood ! To himself he eateth and drinketh
Death and doom ! And from this, preserve us, thou heavenly Father!
Are ye ready, ye children, to eat of the bread of Atonement ?"
Thus with emotion he asked, and together an-swered the children
Yes! with deep sobs interrupted. Then read he the due supplications,
Read the Form of Communion, and in chimed the organ and anthem ;
O! Holy Lamb of God, who takest away our transgressions,
Hear us ! give us thy peace ! have mercy, have mercy upon *us*!
Th' old man, with trembling hand, and heavenly pearls on his eyelids,

Filled now the chalice and paten, and dealt round the mystical symbols.
O! then seemed it to me, as if God, with the broad eye of mid-day,
Clearer looked in at the windows, and all the trees in the churchyard
Bowed down their summits of green, and the grass on the graves 'gan to shiver.

But in the children, (I noted it well; I knew it) there ran a
Tremor of holy rapture along through their icy-cold members.
Decked like an altar before them, there stood the green earth, and above it
Heaven opened itself, as of old before Stephen; there saw they
Radiant in glory the Father, and on his right hand the Redeemer.
Under them hear they the clang of harpstrings, and angels from gold clouds
Beckon to them like brothers, and fan with their pinions of purple.

Closed was the Teacher's task, and with heaven in their hearts and their faces,
Up rose the children all, and each bowed him, weeping full sorely,
Downward to kiss that reverend hand, but all of them pressed he
Moved to his bosom, and laid, with a prayer, his hands full of blessings,
Now on the holy breast, and now on the inno-cent tresses.

THE VILLAGE BLACKSMITH.

UNDER a spreading chestnut tree
The village smithy stands;
   The smith, a mighty man is he,
With large and sinewy hands ;
And the muscles of his brawny arms
Are strong as iron bands.
His hair is crisp, and black, and long,
His face is like the tan;
His brow is wet with honest sweat,
He earns whate'er he can,
And looks the whole world in the face,
For he owes not any man.

Week in, week out, from morn till night,
You can hear his bellows blow;
You can hear him swing his heavy sledge,
With measured beat and slow,
Like a sexton ringing the village bell,
When the evening sun is low.

And children coming home from school
Look in at the open door ;
They love to see the flaming forge,
And hear the bellows roar,
And catch the burning sparks that fly
Like chaff from a threshing floor.
He goes on Sunday to the church,
And sits among his boys ;
He hears the parson pray and preach,
He hears his daughter's voice,
Singing in the village choir,
And it makes his heart rejoice.

It sounds to him like her mother's voice,
Singing in Paradise !
He needs must think of her once more,
How in the grave she lies;
And. with his hard, rough hand he wipes
A tear out of his eyes.

Toiling, — rejoicing, —sorrowing,
Onward through life he goes ;
Each morning sees some task begin,
Each evening sees it close;
Something.attempted, something done,

Has earned a night's repose.
Thanks, thanks to thee, my worthy friend,
For the lesson thou hast taught!
Thus at the flaming forge of life
Our fortunes must be wrought;
Thus on its sounding anvil shaped
Each burning deed and thought!

ENDYMION.
THE rising moon has hid the stars ;
Her level rays, like golden bars.,
Lie on the landscape green,
With shadows brown between.

And silver white the river gleams,
As if Diana, in her dreams,
Had dropt her silver bow
Upon the meadows low.

On such a tranquil night as this,
She woke Endymion with a kiss,
When, sleeping in the grove,
He dreamed not of her love.

Like Dian's kiss, unasked, unsought,
Love gives itself, but is not bought;
Nor voice, nor sound betrays
Its deep, impassioned gaze.

It comes,—the beautiful, the free,
The crown of all humanity, —
In silence and alone
To seek the elected one.

It lifts the boughs, whose shadows deep,
Are Life's oblivion, the soul's sleep,
And kisses the closed eyes
Of him, who slumbering lies.

ENDYMION.

O, weary hearts! O, slumbering eyes!
O, drooping souls, whose destinies
Are fraught with fear and pain,
Ye shall be loved again!

No one is so accursed by fate,
No one so utterly desolate,
But some heart, though unknown,
Responds unto his own.

Responds,-as if with unseen wings,
A breath from heaven had touched its strings;
And whispers, in its song,
"Where hast thou stayed so long!"

THE TWO LOCKS OF HAIR.
FROM THE GERMAN OF PFIZER.

A YOUTH, light-hearted and content,
I wander through the world ;
Here, Arab-like, is pitched my tent
And straight again is furled.

Yet oft I dream, that once a wife

Close in my heart was locked,
And in the sweet repose of life
A blessed child I rocked.

I wake ! Away that dream, — away !
Too long did it remain !
So long, that both by night and day
It ever comes again.

The end lies ever in my thought;
To a grave so cold and deep
The mother beautiful was brought;
Then dropt the child asleep.

But now the dream is wholly o'er,
I bathe mine eyes and see ;
And wander through the world once more,
A youth so light and free.

Two locks,—and they are wondrous fair,—
Left me that vision mild;
The brown is from the mother's hair,
The blond is from the child.

And when I see that lock of gold
Pale grows the evening-red ;
And when the dark lock I behold,
I wish that I were dead.

IT IS NOT ALWAYS MAY.
NO HAY PAJAROS EN LOS NID0S DE AHTANO.

Spanish Proverb.

THE sun is bright,—the air is clear,
The darting swallows soar and sing,
And from the stately elms I hear
The blue-bird prophesying Spring.

So blue yon winding river flows,
It seems an outlet from the sky,
Where waiting till the west wind blows,
The freighted clouds at anchor lie.

All things are new ; the buds, the leaves
That gild the elm-tree's nodding crest,
And even the nest beneath the eaves ; —
There are no birds in last year's nest!

All things rejoice in youth and love,
The fulness of their first delight!
And learn from the soft heavens above
The melting tenderness of night.
Maiden, that read'st this simple rhyme,
Enjoy thy youth, it will not stay;
Enjoy the fragrance of thy prime,
For O! it is not always May !

Enjoy the Spring of Love and Youth,
To some good angel leave the rest;

For Time will teach thee soon the truth,
There are no birds in last year's nest!

THE RAINY DAY.

THE day is cold, and dark, and dreary;
It rains, and the wind is never weary;
The vine still clings to the mouldering wall,
But at every gust the dead leaves fall,
And the day is dark and dreary.

My life is cold, and dark, and dreary;
It rains, and the wind is never weary ;
My thoughts still cling to the mouldering Past,
But the hopes of youth fall thick in the blast
And the days are dark and dreary.

Be still, sad heart! and cease repining;
Behind the clouds is the sun still shining ;
Thy fate is the common fate of all,
Into each life some rain must fall,
Some days must be dark and dreary.

GOD'S-ACRE.

I LIKE that ancient Saxon phrase, which calls
The burial-ground God's-Acre! It is just;
It consecrates each grave within its walls,
And breathes a benison o'er the sleeping dust

God's-Acre ! Yes, that blessed name imparts
Comfort to those, who in the grave have sown

The seed, that they had garnered in their hearts,
Their bread of life, alas! no more their own.

Into its furrows shall we all be cast,
In the sure faith, that we shall rise again
At the great harvest, when the arch-angel's blast
Shall winnow, like a fan, the chaff and grain.

Then shall the good stand in immortal bloom,
In the fair gardens of that second birth;
And each bright blossom, mingle its perfume
With that of flowers, which never bloomed on earth.

With thy rude ploughshare, Death, turn up the sod,
And spread the furrow for the seed we sow;
This is the field and Acre of our God.
This is the place, where human harvests grow!

RIVER! that in silence windest
Through the meadows, bright and free,
Till at length thy rest thou findest
In the bosom of the sea!

Four long years of mingled feeling,
Half in rest, and half in strife,
I have seen thy waters stealing
Onward, like the stream of life.

Thou has taught me, Silent River!
Many a lesson, deep and long; Thou hast been a generous giver;
I can give thee but a song.

Oft in sadness and in illness,

I have watched thy current glide,
Till the beauty of its stillness
Overflowed me, like a tide.

And in better hours and brighter,
When I saw thy waters gleam,
I have felt my heart beat lighter,
And leap onward with thy stream

Not for this alone I love thee,
Nor because, thy waves of blue
From celestial seas above thee
Take their own celestial hue.

Where yon shadowy woodlands hide thee,
And thy waters disappear,
Friends I love have dwelt beside thee,
And have made thy margin dear.

More than this ; — thy name reminds me
Of three friends, all true and tried ;
And that name, like magic, binds me
Closet, closer to thy side.

Friends my soul with joy remembers !
How like quivering flames they start,
When I fan the living embers
On the hearth-stone of my heart!

'T is for this, thou Silent River!
That my spirit leans to thee;.
Thou hast been a generous giver,
Take this idle song from me.

BLIND Bartimeus at the gates
Of Jericho in darkness waits;
He hears the crowd ;—he hears a breath
Say, "It is Christ of Nazareth! "
And calls, in tones of agony,
Inoov enenoov ue!

The thronging multitudes increase ;
Blind Bartimeus, hold thy peace !
But still, above the noisy crowd,
The beggar's cry is shrill and loud ;
 Until they say, " He calleth thee !"

Then saith the Christ, as silent stands
The crowd, " What wilt thou at my hands ?"
And he replies, " O give me light!
Rabbi, restore the blind man's sight!" And Jesus answers,"

Ye that have eyes, yet cannot see;
In darkness and in misery,
Recall those mighty Voices Three,

THE GOBLET OF LIFE.

FILLED is Life's goblet to the brim;
And though my eyes with tears are dint,
I see its sparkling bubbles swim,
And chaunt a melancholy hymn
With solemn voice and slow.

No purple flowers,—no garlands green,

Conceal the goblet's shade or sheen,
Nor maddening draughts of Hippocrene,
Like gleams of sunshine, flash between
Thick leaves of misletoe.

This goblet, wrought with curious art,
Is filled with waters, that upstart,
When the deep fountains of the heart,
By strong convulsions rent apart,
Are running all to waste.

And as it mantling passes round,
With fennel is it wreathed and crowned,
Whose seed and foliage sun-imbrowned
Are in its waters steeped and drowned,
And give a bitter taste.

It gave new strength, and fearless mood ;
And gladiators, fierce and rude,
Mingled it in their daily food;
And he who battled and subdued,
A wreath of fennel wore.

Then in Life's goblet freely press,
The leaves that give it bitterness,
Nor prize the colored waters less,
For in thy darkness and distress
New light and strength they give !

The prayer of Ajax was for light;
Through all that dark and desperate fight,
The blackness of that noonday night,
He asked but the return of sight,

To see his foeman's face.

Let our unceasing, earnest prayer
Be, too, for light, — for strength to bear
Our portion of the weight of care,
That crushes into dumb despair
One half the human race.

I pledge you in this cup of grief,
Where floats the fennel's bitter leaf!
The Battle of our Life is brief,
The alarm, — the struggle, — the relief, Then sleep we side by side.

MAIDENHOOD.

MAIDEN ! with the meek, brown eyes,
In whose orbs a shadow lies
Like the dusk in evening skies !

Thou whose locks outshine the sun,
Golden tresses, wreathed in one,
As the braided streamlets run !

Standing, with reluctant feet,
Where the brook and river meet,
Womanhood and childhood fleet!

Gazing, with a timid glance,
On the brooklet's swift advance,
On the river's broad expanse!

Deep and still, that gliding stream
Beautiful to thee must seem,

As the river of a dream.

Then why pause with indecision,
When bright angels in thy vision
Beckon thee to fields Elysian ?

Seest thou shadows sailing by,
As the dove, with startled eye,
Sees the falcon's shadow fly ?

Hearest thou voices on the shore,
That our ears perceive no more,
Deafened by the cataract's roar ?

O, thou child of many prayers!
Life hath quicksands, — Life hath snare
Care and age come unawares !

Like the swell of some sweet tune, Morning rises into noon, May glides onward into June.
Childhood is the bough, where slumbered
Birds and blossoms many-numbered ; —
Age, that bough with snows encumbered

Gather, then, each flower that grows, When the young heart overflows, To embalm that tent of snows.
Bear a lily in thy hand ;
Gates of brass cannot withstand
One touch of that magic wand.

Bear through sorrow, wrong, and ruth,
In thy heart the dew of youth,
On thy lips the smile of truth.

O, that dew, like balm, shall steal
Into wounds, that cannot heal,
Even as sleep our eyes doth seal;

And that smile, like sunshine, dart
Into many a sunless heart,
For a smile of God thou art.

EXCELSIOR.

THE shades of night were falling fast,
As through an Alpine village passed
A youth, who bore, 'mid snow and ice,
A banner with the strange device Excelsior!

In happy homes he saw the light
Of household fires gleam warm and bright;
Above, the spectral glaciers shone,
And from his lips escaped a groan, Excelsior!

" Try not the Pass !" the old man said ;
" Dark lowers the tempest overhead,
The roaring torrent is deep and wide ! "
And loud that clarion voice replied Excelsior!

" Beware the pine-tree's withered branch!
Beware the awful avalanch! "
This was the peasant's last Good-night,
A voice replied, far up the height,
Excelsior!

At break of day, as heavenward

The pious monks of Saint Bernard
Uttered the oft-repeated prayer,
A voice cried through the startled air Excelsior!

There in the twilight cold and gray,
Lifeless, but beautiful, he lay,
And from the sky, serene and far,
A voice fell, like a falling star,
Execelisor

www.bookjungle.com *email: sales@bookjungle.com fax: 630-214-0564 mail: Book Jungle PO Box 2226 Champaign, IL 61825*

The Codes Of Hammurabi And Moses
W. W. Davies

QTY

The discovery of the Hammurabi Code is one of the greatest achievements of archaeology, and is of paramount interest, not only to the student of the Bible, but also to all those interested in ancient history...

Religion ISBN: *1-59462-338-4* Pages:132
MSRP *$12.95*

The Theory of Moral Sentiments
Adam Smith

QTY

This work from 1749. contains original theories of conscience amd moral judgment and it is the foundation for systemof morals.

Philosophy ISBN: *1-59462-777-0* Pages:536
MSRP *$19.95*

Jessica's First Prayer
Hesba Stretton

QTY

In a screened and secluded corner of one of the many railway-bridges which span the streets of London there could be seen a few years ago, from five o'clock every morning until half past eight, a tidily set-out coffee-stall, consisting of a trestle and board, upon which stood two large tin cans, with a small fire of charcoal burning under each so as to keep the coffee boiling during the early hours of the morning when the work-people were thronging into the city on their way to their daily toil...

Childrens ISBN: *1-59462-373-2* Pages:84
MSRP *$9.95*

My Life and Work
Henry Ford

QTY

Henry Ford revolutionized the world with his implementation of mass production for the Model T automobile. Gain valuable business insight into his life and work with his own auto-biography... "We have only started on our development of our country we have not as yet, with all our talk of wonderful progress, done more than scratch the surface. The progress has been wonderful enough but..."

Biographies/ ISBN: *1-59462-198-5* Pages:300
MSRP *$21.95*

www.bookjungle.com email: sales@bookjungle.com fax: 630-214-0564 mail: Book Jungle PO Box 2226 Champaign, IL 61825

The Art of Cross-Examination
Francis Wellman

QTY

I presume it is the experience of every author, after his first book is published upon an important subject, to be almost overwhelmed with a wealth of ideas and illustrations which could readily have been included in his book, and which to his own mind, at least, seem to make a second edition inevitable. Such certainly was the case with me; and when the first edition had reached its sixth impression in five months, I rejoiced to learn that it seemed to my publishers that the book had met with a sufficiently favorable reception to justify a second and considerably enlarged edition. ..

Reference   ISBN: *1-59462-647-2*   Pages:412   MSRP $19.95

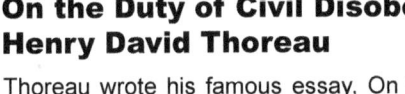

On the Duty of Civil Disobedience
Henry David Thoreau

QTY

Thoreau wrote his famous essay, On the Duty of Civil Disobedience, as a protest against an unjust but popular war and the immoral but popular institution of slave-owning. He did more than write—he declined to pay his taxes, and was hauled off to gaol in consequence. Who can say how much this refusal of his hastened the end of the war and of slavery ?

Law   ISBN: *1-59462-747-9*   Pages:48   MSRP $7.45

Dream Psychology Psychoanalysis for Beginners
Sigmund Freud

QTY

Sigmund Freud, born Sigismund Schlomo Freud (May 6, 1856 - September 23, 1939), was a Jewish-Austrian neurologist and psychiatrist who co-founded the psychoanalytic school of psychology. Freud is best known for his theories of the unconscious mind, especially involving the mechanism of repression; his redefinition of sexual desire as mobile and directed towards a wide variety of objects; and his therapeutic techniques, especially his understanding of transference in the therapeutic relationship and the presumed value of dreams as sources of insight into unconscious desires.

Psychology   ISBN: *1-59462-905-6*   Pages:196   MSRP $15.45

The Miracle of Right Thought
Orison Swett Marden

QTY

Believe with all of your heart that you will do what you were made to do. When the mind has once formed the habit of holding cheerful, happy, prosperous pictures, it will not be easy to form the opposite habit. It does not matter how improbable or how far away this realization may see, or how dark the prospects may be, if we visualize them as best we can, as vividly as possible, hold tenaciously to them and vigorously struggle to attain them, they will gradually become actualized, realized in the life. But a desire, a longing without endeavor, a yearning abandoned or held indifferently will vanish without realization.

Self Help   ISBN: *1-59462-644-8*   Pages:360   MSRP $25.45

www.bookjungle.com *email: sales@bookjungle.com fax: 630-214-0564 mail: Book Jungle PO Box 2226 Champaign, IL 61825*

QTY

- [ ] **The Rosicrucian Cosmo-Conception Mystic Christianity** *by Max Heindel* ISBN: *1-59462-188-8* **$38.95**
  The Rosicrucian Cosmo-conception is not dogmatic, neither does it appeal to any other authority than the reason of the student. It is: not controversial, but is: sent forth in the, hope that it may help to clear... New Age/Religion Pages 646

- [ ] **Abandonment To Divine Providence** *by Jean-Pierre de Caussade* ISBN: *1-59462-228-0* **$25.95**
  "The Rev. Jean Pierre de Caussade was one of the most remarkable spiritual writers of the Society of Jesus in France in the 18th Century. His death took place at Toulouse in 1751. His works have gone through many editions and have been republished..." Inspirational/Religion Pages 400

- [ ] **Mental Chemistry** *by Charles Haanel* ISBN: *1-59462-192-6* **$23.95**
  Mental Chemistry allows the change of material conditions by combining and appropriately utilizing the power of the mind. Much like applied chemistry creates something new and unique out of careful combinations of chemicals the mastery of mental chemistry... New Age Pages 354

- [ ] **The Letters of Robert Browning and Elizabeth Barret Barrett 1845-1846 vol II** ISBN: *1-59462-193-4* **$35.95**
  by Robert Browning and Elizabeth Barrett Biographies Pages 596

- [ ] **Gleanings In Genesis (volume I)** *by Arthur W. Pink* ISBN: *1-59462-130-6* **$27.45**
  Appropriately has Genesis been termed "the seed plot of the Bible" for in it we have, in germ form, almost all of the great doctrines which are afterwards fully developed in the books of Scripture which follow... Religion/Inspirational Pages 420

- [ ] **The Master Key** *by L. W. de Laurence* ISBN: *1-59462-001-6* **$30.95**
  In no branch of human knowledge has there been a more lively increase of the spirit of research during the past few years than in the study of Psychology, Concentration and Mental Discipline. The requests for authentic lessons in Thought Control, Mental Discipline and... New Age/Business Pages 422

- [ ] **The Lesser Key Of Solomon Goetia** *by L. W. de Laurence* ISBN: *1-59462-092-X* **$9.95**
  This translation of the first book of the "Lernegton" which is now for the first time made accessible to students of Talismanic Magic was done, after careful collation and edition, from numerous Ancient Manuscripts in Hebrew, Latin, and French... New Age/Occult Pages 92

- [ ] **Rubaiyat Of Omar Khayyam** *by Edward Fitzgerald* ISBN:*1-59462-332-5* **$13.95**
  Edward Fitzgerald, whom the world has already learned, in spite of his own efforts to remain within the shadow of anonymity, to look upon as one of the rarest poets of the century, was born at Bredfield, in Suffolk, on the 31st of March, 1809. He was the third son of John Purcell... Music Pages 172

- [ ] **Ancient Law** *by Henry Maine* ISBN: *1-59462-128-4* **$29.95**
  The chief object of the following pages is to indicate some of the earliest ideas of mankind, as they are reflected in Ancient Law, and to point out the relation of those ideas to modern thought. Religiom/History Pages 452

- [ ] **Far-Away Stories** *by William J. Locke* ISBN: *1-59462-129-2* **$19.45**
  "Good wine needs no bush, but a collection of mixed vintages does. And this book is just such a collection. Some of the stories I do not want to remain buried for ever in the museum files of dead magazine-numbers an author's not unpardonable vanity..." Fiction Pages 272

- [ ] **Life of David Crockett** *by David Crockett* ISBN: *1-59462-250-7* **$27.45**
  "Colonel David Crockett was one of the most remarkable men of the times in which he lived. Born in humble life, but gifted with a strong will, an indomitable courage, and unremitting perseverance... Biographies/New Age Pages 424

- [ ] **Lip-Reading** *by Edward Nitchie* ISBN: *1-59462-206-X* **$25.95**
  Edward B. Nitchie, founder of the New York School for the Hard of Hearing, now the Nitchie School of Lip-Reading, Inc, wrote "LIP-READING Principles and Practice". The development and perfecting of this meritorious work on lip-reading was an undertaking... How-to Pages 400

- [ ] **A Handbook of Suggestive Therapeutics, Applied Hypnotism, Psychic Science** ISBN: *1-59462-214-0* **$24.95**
  by Henry Munro Health/New Age/Health/Self-help Pages 376

- [ ] **A Doll's House: and Two Other Plays** *by Henrik Ibsen* ISBN: *1-59462-112-8* **$19.95**
  Henrik Ibsen created this classic when in revolutionary 1848 Rome. Introducing some striking concepts in playwriting for the realist genre, this play has been studied the world over. Fiction/Classics/Plays 308

- [ ] **The Light of Asia** *by sir Edwin Arnold* ISBN: *1-59462-204-3* **$13.95**
  In this poetic masterpiece, Edwin Arnold describes the life and teachings of Buddha. The man who was to become known as Buddha to the world was born as Prince Gautama of India but he rejected the worldly riches and abandoned the reigns of power when... Religion/History/Biographies Pages 170

- [ ] **The Complete Works of Guy de Maupassant** *by Guy de Maupassant* ISBN: *1-59462-157-8* **$16.95**
  "For days and days, nights and nights, I had dreamed of that first kiss which was to consecrate our engagement, and I knew not on what spot I should put my lips..." Fiction/Classics Pages 240

- [ ] **The Art of Cross-Examination** *by Francis L. Wellman* ISBN: *1-59462-309-0* **$26.95**
  Written by a renowned trial lawyer, Wellman imparts his experience and uses case studies to explain how to use psychology to extract desired information through questioning. How-to/Science/Reference Pages 408

- [ ] **Answered or Unanswered?** *by Louisa Vaughan* ISBN: *1-59462-248-5* **$10.95**
  Miracles of Faith in China Religion Pages 112

- [ ] **The Edinburgh Lectures on Mental Science (1909)** *by Thomas* ISBN: *1-59462-008-3* **$11.95**
  This book contains the substance of a course of lectures recently given by the writer in the Queen Street Hail, Edinburgh. Its purpose is to indicate the Natural Principles governing the relation between Mental Action and Material Conditions... New Age/Psychology Pages 148

- [ ] **Ayesha** *by H. Rider Haggard* ISBN: *1-59462-301-5* **$24.95**
  Verily and indeed it is the unexpected that happens! Probably if there was one person upon the earth from whom the Editor of this, and of a certain previous history, did not expect to hear again... Classics Pages 380

- [ ] **Ayala's Angel** *by Anthony Trollope* ISBN: *1-59462-352-X* **$29.95**
  The two girls were both pretty, but Lucy who was twenty-one who supposed to be simple and comparatively unattractive, whereas Ayala was credited, as her Bombwhat romantic name might show, with poetic charm and a taste for romance. Ayala when her father died was nineteen... Fiction Pages 484

- [ ] **The American Commonwealth** *by James Bryce* ISBN: *1-59462-286-8* **$34.45**
  An interpretation of American democratic political theory. It examines political mechanics and society from the perspective of Scotsman James Bryce Politics Pages 572

- [ ] **Stories of the Pilgrims** *by Margaret P. Pumphrey* ISBN: *1-59462-116-0* **$17.95**
  This book explores pilgrims religious oppression in England as well as their escape to Holland and eventual crossing to America on the Mayflower, and their early days in New England... History Pages 268

www.bookjungle.com email: sales@bookjungle.com fax: 630-214-0564 mail: Book Jungle PO Box 2226 Champaign, IL 61825

QTY

The Fasting Cure *by Sinclair Upton*   ISBN: *1-59462-222-1* $13.95
In the Cosmopolitan Magazine for May, 1910, and in the Contemporary Review (London) for April, 1910, I published an article dealing with my experiences in fasting. I have written a great many magazine articles, but never one which attracted so much attention... *New Age/Self Help/Health Pages 164*

Hebrew Astrology *by Sepharial*   ISBN: *1-59462-308-2* $13.45
In these days of advanced thinking it is a matter of common observation that we have left many of the old landmarks behind and that we are now pressing forward to greater heights and to a wider horizon than that which represented the mind-content of our progenitors... *Astrology Pages 144*

Thought Vibration or The Law of Attraction in the Thought World   ISBN: *1-59462-127-6* $12.95
by William Walker Atkinson   *Psychology/Religion Pages 144*

Optimism *by Helen Keller*   ISBN: *1-59462-108-X* $15.95
Helen Keller was blind, deaf, and mute since 19 months old, yet famously learned how to overcome these handicaps, communicate with the world, and spread her lectures promoting optimism. An inspiring read for everyone... *Biographies/Inspirational Pages 84*

Sara Crewe *by Frances Burnett*   ISBN: *1-59462-360-0* $9.45
In the first place, Miss Minchin lived in London. Her home was a large, dull, tall one, in a large, dull square, where all the houses were alike, and all the sparrows were alike, and where all the door-knockers made the same heavy sound... *Childrens/Classic Pages 88*

The Autobiography of Benjamin Franklin *by Benjamin Franklin*   ISBN: *1-59462-135-7* $24.95
The Autobiography of Benjamin Franklin has probably been more extensively read than any other American historical work, and no other book of its kind has had such ups and downs of fortune. Franklin lived for many years in England, where he was agent... *Biographies/History Pages 332*

Name	
Email	
Telephone	
Address	
City, State ZIP	

☐ Credit Card   ☐ Check / Money Order

Credit Card Number	
Expiration Date	
Signature	

Please Mail to: Book Jungle
                   PO Box 2226
                   Champaign, IL 61825
or Fax to: 630-214-0564

ORDERING INFORMATION

web: *www.bookjungle.com*
email: *sales@bookjungle.com*
fax: *630-214-0564*
mail: *Book Jungle PO Box 2226 Champaign, IL 61825*
or PayPal *to sales@bookjungle.com*

Please contact us for bulk discounts

DIRECT-ORDER TERMS

**20% Discount if You Order
Two or More Books**
Free Domestic Shipping!
Accepted: Master Card, Visa,
Discover, American Express

www.ingramcontent.com/pod-product-compliance
Lightning Source LLC
Chambersburg PA
CBHW081330040426
42453CB00013B/2363